PHILOSOPHY FOR ALIENS

An examination of philosophy from an alien or universal perspective, featuring the unavoidable limits to possible knowledge, limits that constitute 'a philosophical black hole'.

The author acknowledges assistance from Russell Berg, Janis Entwisle, Arthur Haigh, Guy Otten and Louise Robinson.

British Library Cataloguing in Publication Data.
A catalogue record for this book is available from the British Library.

ISBN 978-0-9575540-0-9

Published by Intellect Publishing – P.O. Box 427, Manchester M45 0BA. United Kingdom.

Printed and bound by CPI Group (UK) Ltd, Croydon, CR0 4YY

PHILOSOPHY FOR ALIENS

GEOFFREY BERG

Discovering 'The Philosophical Black Hole'

CONTENTS

INTRODUCTION

In this book I invite you to imagine you are an extra-terrestrial, an extraterrestrial philosopher.

In ages past I might have asked you to imagine you were a Martian philosopher living on Mars. However as astronomers have now found the chances of intelligent life existing on Mars are negligible, I invite you to imagine you are a philosopher from some alien life form existing on some faraway planet orbiting a distant star. Still the principle is the same and the objective is the same. The real objective is to separate out what in the subject matter of philosophy is truly universal for all entities in the Universe from what is essentially 'humancentric' or anthropocentric (I prefer to use the word 'humancentric'). So we will try to separate out in the subject of philosophy the universal, indeed 'the necessarily universal' from the ephemeral and localised concerns of mankind. In that way we may be able to reach some universal truths, indeed some necessarily universal truths applicable to everything, everything in the Universe (or even 'multiverse') as distinct from what derives just from human circumstances and human outlooks.

I don't know whether any past or present philosopher has examined philosophy and tested philosophical theories in these terms. However, I do know that no preeminent philosopher has ever done so in their main books on philosophy. That will not deter me from doing so. Indeed it will simplify matters because I will not need to refer much to other philosophers. It will also help me to keep the language and concepts I use relatively simple. I have also broken up many of the paragraphs I used in my first draft of this book to make the book easier to read. To make up for now sometimes splitting the flow of the argument I have introduced subtitles and blank lines between some paragraphs to correspond with natural breaks in the lines of thought or arguments. This should make it possible (albeit not always easy) for even relatively intelligent people, educated in any subject to understand what I am saying. Incidentally I am not myself claiming to have any great expertise nor even great interest in most aspects of philosophy, just a general knowledge and some real insight that comes from taking a very fresh view of matters.

So the first striking feature of this book is the attempt to view philosophy or philosophical questions not primarily from a human point of view but, at least hypothetically, from the viewpoint of an alien life form or extra-terrestrial.

The second striking feature is that I try to demonstrate from both a human and an alien perspective a great ultimate disintegration in much general philosophy and particularly concerning ultimate universal questions. There is a kind of 'philosophical black hole' at the core of philosophy that one encounters if one is serious about philosophy before one gets to answers for many of the main philosophical questions. This is a philosophical black hole one must fall into beyond a certain point and one just cannot get to the other side of it and out of it. So the second big theme of this book and this also is a novel theme, is that there necessarily is an intellectual disintegration or black hole that is the final stage one (be one human or extra-terrestrial) can reach in many aspects of philosophy. This is certainly applicable so far as most truly universal questions are concerned. One may ask is this all just a consequence of the Logic that I and humans generally use? Does this not indicate a fault in our Logic rather than a necessary philosophical 'great disintegration' or 'philosophical black hole'? I do consider that question and my emphatic answer is no. If we cannot rely on some Logic, then the only reason we may not get to 'the great disintegration' I speak of is because we may not get anywhere at all in respect of most 'philosophical questions' or 'real underlying knowledge'.

So I maintain there is a 'philosophical black hole' or 'great disintegration of philosophy' at the centre or core of philosophy that swallows up everything before one has reached ultimate answers to so many questions. This 'philosophical black hole' is in many ways akin to the supposed astronomical black hole at the centre of our galaxy.

I think it is practically unaccountable and truly incredible that this 'philosophical black hole' has apparently never been noticed nor publicised by any major philosopher nor by any philosopher of whom I am aware. That however will not prevent me from expounding these universal truths as I see them.

So I will examine each significant part of philosophy, first from the point of view of whether there can be proper answers to the questions that are raised or whether it inevitably falls into a 'great disintegration' in philosophy or philosophical black hole. Then I will examine each major part of philosophy from an alien perspective to determine whether that subject matter is essentially universal or otherwise specific to certain types of life form such as people. From such examinations and from such novel perspectives some new universal and philosophical truths should become apparent.

PART I - The Great Disintegration of Ultimate Knowledge and Much Philosophy.

Chapter 1: Values, Goodness and Beauty

Perhaps the greatest concern of philosophers, certainly of many philosophers including the greatest classical philosophers, Plato (c428-c348BC) and Aristotle (384-322BC) was about values in general, and most particularly to discover what constitutes 'the good life'. This search continues both among philosophers and also the wider public but there is no real agreement and certainly no consensus. Even the so called golden rule, 'do unto others what you would have done to yourself' does not take us very far - apart from in any event upon close examination not being strictly speaking sensible. After all people are different and different people have different likes and dislikes. For instance some people like to travel or live riskily while others do not. Some people like to receive little gifts while others would find that insulting.

Good and Bad

Even among humans, let alone among all life forms on Earth (let alone in the Universe as a whole) it is so difficult as to be practically impossible to state precisely what 'good' or 'goodness' is. Yet people in general do talk of 'good' and 'bad'. The problem comes not with our capacity to talk of good and bad. It is not even with people having a vague common understanding of 'good' and 'bad', especially in relation to individual instances of 'good' and 'bad'. The problem is with our widespread incapacity to properly analyse 'good' and 'bad' and find a general substantive grounding for good and bad.

This surely suggests that human notions of good and bad derive from either human instinct or human societal needs rather than from any proper analysis or understanding of ultimate reality. So could it be that 'good' and 'bad' are just artificial notions that happen to be useful to humanity derived either from our instinct or from our upbringing rather than from real features of the Universe that exist independently of us? I think so. Analysis rather shows that when tested against and set into the context of absolute reality the concept of goodness just vanishes and falls into what I term 'the great philosophical disintegration' akin to a philosophical black hole.

So I grant that people generally are, and it is widely thought ought to be brought up with a notion of right and wrong and develop the ability to distinguish 'right' from 'wrong' in various contexts. That is evidently and undoubtedly true and actually useful from the point of view of general human wellbeing. It is after all important in terms of our ability to live and prosper through controlling our environment while not damaging each other daily for people (like, more primitively, lions) to live in a society or group. That also enables humans to specialise in tasks (for instance originally men in hunting or working, women in home keeping and rearing children) and so look after dependent children and sick and elderly people. This has over time been extended by job differentiation and ever more specialisation in human knowledge and activities. For all this a grouping or society of individuals is essential.

So what is important in behavioural terms for a society to function well can come to be seen as 'good'. This sometimes (though not in fact always) means voluntarily sacrificing individual interests (such as say sharing food rather than having the ablest grab most food) for the benefit of others in that society. This is a societal benefit (or in loose terms 'good') rather than a universal good. Similarly, to take one example, a well organised society will farm land to produce food for itself. Yet it is not of any universal value in the universal scheme of things that there is wheat rather than grass or shrub in some land on Earth, or that cattle rather than rabbits and wolves populate land. After all though that may be good for cattle (if being reared to be milked or eaten can be termed 'good') it is no use nor good at all for the rabbits and wolves who would otherwise live there. So what I am saying is what we humans term 'good' is not a metaphysical nor a universal good nor even necessarily 'good' in terms of any particular individual human.

What we call 'good' is generally a term denoting 'useful for some human society'. It is a little akin to, even though not exactly the same as 'the greatest good for the greatest number'. Even within this perspective there are indeed different and sometimes conflicting understandings of what exactly constitutes this utilitarian type good. For instance people think differently to some extent in terms of whether good is more akin to justice (giving everybody their just deserts) or to benevolence (taking a kindly, benevolent view for everybody). There is even more division of views as between how much society overall benefits from giving free rein to individuals and individualism which gives advantages to the strong (to gain wealth, power, freedom or prestige) rather than from suppressing individualism to make things 'fairer' for all. For instance how much are incentives (in money etc) needed (and therefore become 'good') to motivate individuals to work harder, longer or with more ability (such as in being doctors) than others? So if one analyses thoroughly even our everyday notions of 'good', couched merely in terms of utility or usefulness, let alone supposedly universal concepts of good, it ends up becoming vague, unclear and probably indeterminable.

As to whether human notions of 'good' are essentially instinctive (as flying is for birds) or developed environmentally with the guidance of parents, or a combination of the two I am unable to say. Yet that they are generally rather utilitarian and not reflective of any universal good is evident upon analysis. Values do not pervade the Universe. In universal terms what is beneficial (and so in shorthand 'good') for some things and helps such things prosper is also generally correspondingly harmful (and therefore in shorthand 'bad') for other things that either exist or would in other circumstances have existed. Therefore there is surely no universal 'good' permeating the Universe.

I suppose romantics (contrary to a Taoist view) might argue that advanced intelligences, especially those that spread 'civilisation' are good for the Universe. Likewise I suppose some would argue that the British Empire, or at least the supposedly positive aspects of the British Empire was good for the world, though it certainly was never good for everybody or everything! Indeed 'action' generally results in change, change which is 'good' for some things but conversely must be worse for other things (that are either changed or diminished).

Even the mere spread of knowledge if it is to mean anything in actuality results in such change. What then of the notion of abstract knowledge or awareness being an absolute 'good' or 'virtue'? Apart from the possibility that it might bring sorrow about the nature of things (such as knowing about death apparently does to humans and maybe elephants), it is hard to argue in absolute terms that it is better rather than just different to ignorance.

Anyhow in universal terms all living things, all conscious entities are ephemeral and probably none of them are ever dominant over the whole Universe. Indeed I say the Universe is most accurately described as an implacable, abstract ever changing pattern of things, a pattern without feelings and without values permeating inherently throughout it. This even applies to the concepts of 'pain' and 'painlessness' which is a common aspect of the notion of 'good' for humans. I forsake the trivial point that painlessness or at any rate little pain (if pain is useful as a biological warning to a living body) may be 'bad' for the things that cause pain. The real point is it can surely be of no universal concern nor consequence to the overall ever changing pattern of things whether some entities are in pain or not.

So even apart from the impossibility of precisely understanding, defining or knowing what is meant by 'goodness', there is clearly no inherent substantive element of 'good' permeating the Universe or underpinning the Universe. The more closely and the more precisely one examines the concept of 'good' and the value of 'goodness' the more it disintegrates and then vanishes even in terms of humanity, let alone in terms of the Universe as a whole. 'Good' simply evaporates as a meaningful concept in absolute terms. So it falls into 'the great disintegration' which I claim is at the very centre of ultimate philosophical enquiry which brings most parts of philosophy to a complete halt long before universal conclusions are reached.

Beauty

The humancentricity of the notion of beauty and the philosophy of aesthetics should be even more obvious than the humancentricity of people's notions of 'good'. What is said to be beautiful is not a universal nor cosmological feature nor anything that an alien would necessarily agree with - it is just something in the mind of the beholder.

For instance from the point of view of male minds what is beautiful in a female is first a matter of species, then a matter of his pre-determined brain wiring and finally a matter of his individual taste. For example male elephants think female elephants, not female humans, are attractive. Male chimpanzees evidently think some female chimpanzees, not female humans are attractive. It is only male humans who seem to get attracted by human 'female beauty'. Instinctive signals also clearly play a considerable part. In most animals males in general are attracted not especially by a female all the time but by females in the special occasional state of oestrus. Conversely females seem to see male beauty or desirability not merely in terms of natural beauty but in terms of status or 'dominance'.

Furthermore at least among humans research has now shown that certain proportions and symmetry in features are widely seen as more beautiful than other proportions. That derives from human minds and not from one set of proportions relating to physical features being clearly better or more beautiful in universal terms than another set of proportions. Additionally individuals can be quirky. It is not just that males of different human races veer to different opinions of female beauty. Even among males of the same race and family there tend to be different individual views as to what makes a woman individually beautiful.

There is no universal benchmark for nor ultimately correct notion of beauty. Beauty is clearly in essence in the eye of the beholder. This applies not just to sexual beauty but to all types of supposed beauty, be it in architecture, painting or anything else.

Perhaps some would argue that beauty may not just exist in physical form but may come in the mental ability to solve problems - a beautiful mind. A simple solution to a complex problem may often be termed 'beautiful' by humans. Well, apart from aiding comprehensibility, there is no genuine reason why a simple solution to a complex problem should be any more beautiful or inherently any better than a complex solution. Moreover one can properly ask isn't it just a misnomer to call cleverness or some aspect of cleverness beauty? Anyhow couldn't we merely say that some humans are just attuned to liking cleverness just as some humans are naturally attuned to liking eating sugar or playing board games? Maybe camels are more attuned to liking sand and deserts while humans may prefer to look at snow capped mountains and green valleys?

So in universal terms or in terms of absolute universal truth there is no such thing as absolute beauty. How could there be? What can 'beauty' be except some sort of correlation between a mind and its vision of things through the prism of that very same mind complete with its nature and its instincts? How can a thing - beauty - that cannot be satisfactorily defined or even known in universal terms exist universally? This point is reinforced by our knowing that our human notions of beauty exist in alignment with purely human and often individual notions and predispositions!

Researchers may indeed and perhaps profitably (in terms of extending human knowledge) examine the links between human minds and human notions of beauty in physiological terms. However as soon as one begins to think of beauty (or aesthetics) in universal terms that extend beyond humanity, the whole notion rapidly disintegrates into a big philosophical black hole and ends up vanishing entirely.

****

So I am demonstrating that the values and value judgments we humans hold, either individually or as a species, are purely human. Other animals and alien life forms if they make value judgments are likely to hold different values, probably values more suited than human values to their existence and welfare. What any such values are not and cannot be are universal features or essential components of the fabric of the Universe.

Human expressions and notions of 'good' and 'beautiful' are in fact imprecise, sometimes contradictory, perhaps instinctive, mere generalist human shorthand. This shorthand starts to disintegrate and then disappear as concrete concepts when one examines and analyses it carefully even in human terms. If one attempts to cast notions of 'good' or 'beautiful' into universal terms or supposes they are in universal terms in any way part of the very fabric of the Universe, they must disintegrate and vanish entirely down a philosophical black hole.

Values may make some sense in subjective terms but in objective terms there can be no phenomenon in ultimate truth nor ultimate reality concerning values that genuinely exists to underpin them. This becomes apparent when one begins to examine and analyse human values carefully and surely cannot be otherwise in any universalist sense.

Chapter 2: Language, Causality and Knowledge

Now I turn from what are frequently recognised to be subjective topics concerning values to some fundamental things which are usually reckoned to be objectively based rather than merely subjective to different humans. Previously I examined that part of the Philosophy which concerns values, goodness and beauty. Now I will examine the other main part of Philosophy which is concerned to discover the nature of things as they are. Philosophers and indeed scientists in this search into the nature of reality generally aim to achieve objective truth. However I will argue that much of that search after one gets to a certain point beneath the immediate surface necessarily becomes futile as large elements of that topic soon disintegrate, then vanish into a great philosophical black hole.

Language

The first element of knowledge and the first thing most humans learn in any academic sense is language so that they can communicate in a sophisticated, supposedly precise way that takes them beyond the capabilities of animals. Clearly language is very useful. When compounded with book publishing and more latterly computers, language certainly enables people to increase the scope of their expertise and knowledge. It lets people not only record their own experience and knowledge but also to a substantial degree access the accumulated discoveries and knowledge of strangers and even of the dead of previous generations. This is practically necessarily massively useful and massively important to people or for that matter to any entity that has such capabilities. So on the upside language is undoubtedly a massive advantage in communication, most especially when it gets to be written down or recorded for passing on to others. Language is the vehicle or rather the road along which experience and even knowledge can travel.

Unfortunately in much twentieth century philosophy language was seen (via for instance Gottlob Frege 1848-1925, Bertrand Russell 1872-1970 and Ludwig Wittgenstein 1889-1951) not merely as the arterial route along which knowledge travels but as a source of knowledge itself. It may to an extent be true that if you don't have an adequate language, an adequate route for transporting knowledge you are limited in where you can go in your quest for knowledge. You cannot easily travel where there is no road. Likewise where a language is unable to embrace or properly express certain concepts (through lack of vocabulary or perhaps a poor infrastructure) it may not be possible to go to certain places along the route to knowledge. It is also possible that where the usual linguistic modes of expression subsume logical fallacies (as logical positivists claimed), it may be hard to break free of such logical fallacies. In that way one's route to attaining knowledge may indeed be limited or even confused.

However language or the route through which knowledge passes is emphatically not knowledge itself. That is where I fundamentally disagree with the philosophical fashion for linguistic analysis as a key to knowledge which predates Frege (1848-1925) by a long way. It can be found in Plato and many others but became very fashionable after Frege. The real fallacy in linguistic analysis philosophy is to imagine that language has great real precision in usage rather than being just a rough and ready but useful means of communication between ordinary people handed down from generation to generation.

In essence language is not going to be more precise, more rigorous or even in essence much more intelligent or deeply thought out than the ordinary people who use it day by day for mainly ordinary daily matters in their lives. Obviously to an extent correct usage of language is (or perhaps more precisely was) taught in schools and by parents. Obviously language has to be by and large commonly understood and mean roughly the same thing to different people in society to be of much use. Yet in essence language can normally only be a means of expressing reality and not be in itself a determinant of reality itself.

Indeed my view is confirmed by many things I can point to. For instance unlike logical or scientific truth, language changes from time to time - one need only look at a text a few hundred years old to see that English has changed. It has changed not only to accommodate new discoveries and new concepts but also as a result of foreign influences or just mere fashions. Language is also unusual in that if what is at one time an incorrect usage becomes commonplace it eventually becomes the correct and accepted usage. Ultimately the formerly correct usage (via the midway of being an alternative usage) even becomes a wrong usage! Look for instance at the supplanting of f (when pronounced as s) by s or more latterly of z by s in the English version (contrasted with the American version) of English - for instance 'surprize' has over the years become 'surprise'! Furthermore as there are so many different languages in the world (which suggests that language originally developed as a means for merely local communication within smallish tribes or societies) languages can be compared. Languages differ substantially not merely in vocabulary but also in structure, extent and sophistication, as well as often being conceptually different. Surely this on its own would suggest one cannot sensibly hope to find ultimate truth merely by examining our language, as many philosophers, especially recently have supposed.

Yet, as I have indicated, the most important reason why language is a route along which knowledge travels, not an inherent source of knowledge, is its sheer imprecision. Language is best focused when in common use. An analogy could be with a magnifying glass. If you try to examine things from too far or in too much detail with a magnifying glass, focus disappears and far from achieving better vision objects become fuzzy and then indistinguishable. There is an optimum magnification and focus for magnifying glasses for viewing things and either way beyond that optimum setting, the viewing gets worse rather than better and the greater the variance from the optimum the worse it gets. Likewise language is best viewed as an approximate means by which people (and perhaps other entities) can communicate with each other.

When one goes beyond simple concepts people usually neither think precisely, nor still less communicate precisely. Anyhow one person's understanding of most individual words is not precisely (rather than approximately) the same as another person's understanding of those same words. So when one stretches or analyses the meaning of language (which is notoriously often ambiguous anyhow) precision and ultimately meaningfulness starts disappearing. Just to take one example, most people can easily distinguish clear instances of simple colours, say blue and green. Yet once one comes to shades of colours (such as blue, turquoise, green etc) peoples' opinions of what constitutes one colour rather than another colour start to diverge and the consensus of a common language begins to disappear.

There is clearly a limit to the usefulness and even validity of language if we are not speaking a language with precisely the same meanings, which as humans we are not. At that stage language has started to fail even as a means of communicating truth or other things. Language is only at best a description of knowledge and in complex cases not even generally adequate for that when people begin to have slightly different understandings of many words. Language can never be an inherent source of knowledge.

So, as I explained, language is indeed useful as a basic means of common communication and common transmission of ideas or knowledge between us. Indeed language can often still be serviceable and helpful for the transmission of quite complex ideas and notions but if you wish to suppose that there are some deeper metaphysical or even philosophical truths underlying language, forget it. Language has neither enough commonality nor precision for that. Furthermore far from language in itself being an expression of underlying truth, language is merely used to convey a reflection of the language user's own reaction to what he (the language user) actually sees or thinks - i.e. not necessarily what the inherent truth itself is.

So I am saying if language is analysed and examined too closely, far from revealing more truth in general its accuracy and focus will be found to be diminishing, possibly even to the point of uselessness in philosophical if not in everyday terms. Then language will start disintegrating, maybe to the point of falling into the great philosophical black hole I have enunciated. Language of itself is a rough and ready though indeed useful means of communication - it is not itself a source of any substantive or universal truth.

Causality

Let us now turn to examining what has been far more generally, indeed practically universally throughout historical times if not longer, the route to discovering truths - I speak of the nexus of 'causality'. This is the one part of this book where I know some major philosophers, notably David Hume (1711-1776) and before him the ancient Indian Carvakas have actually come to essentially the same conclusion as myself. Perhaps it is a pity that Hume did not seem to analyse the whole of philosophy in the way he in my view correctly analysed 'causality'.

However to put this in my own words, I begin by emphasising the practical importance rather than the theoretical limitations of causality or more precisely 'the nexus of causality'. It is through things, to many minds all things seeming to have causes that humans in general and more narrowly scientists in particular try to make sense of the world and then develop more 'knowledge' about it.

In fact the apparent 'nexus of causality' around it endows our world (perhaps even the Universe) with enough regularity of pattern to make effective and certainly advanced life and living possible. If everything or even most things just happened randomly, life would scarcely be possible. To take just one example, the mere prolonged interposing of layers of dust clouds between the Sun and the Earth in place of the regular pattern of the seasons can definitely make most life on Earth unsustainable. This has actually happened on very rare occasions and through disruption to the regular pattern of crop growth it has killed very many animals and ultimately it could kill practically all advanced life forms. Advanced life, at least of our type, needs great regularity.

The nexus of causality in our region is perhaps the prime vehicle for providing regularity and certainly a rationally comprehensible environment in which people can survive, live and advance via scientific and technological knowledge etc. There could be little effective science or technology if in the world we lived in for instance water sometimes froze at O°C and sometimes froze at 110°C or at any temperature it felt like! We humans can cope with some unpredictability but not with overwhelming nor even predominant unpredictability in either ourselves or our environment. So the nexus of causality is of great use to us and is essential to our development as a race.

The problem comes when one jumps - as is tempting for so many people - from viewing 'causality' as being widespread in our environment to viewing 'causality' as being fundamentally and permanently embedded into the very nature of the Universe. However causality is not and cannot be universal for two reasons. The first reason is that there necessarily cannot ultimately be a cause to everything because of the 'uncaused cause' problem. The second reason is that the nexus of causality can actually break down at any point which even scientists have now recognised through quantum theory and Heisenberg's uncertainty principle.

To turn first to the logic of causality, there cannot be an endless sequence of causality. Causality must logically come to an end at some point. To simplify (because as Aristotle pointed out there can be several kinds of causes) an event such as an injury one suffers is likely to have a cause. That cause may itself have a cause which may itself have a cause but the sequence of causality will end at some point. For instance one may be in a road accident and be injured because a car driver wasn't paying attention. Perhaps he wasn't paying attention because he was distracted by an alcoholic semi-stupor. Perhaps he had got into that stupor because he was socialising with friends because he liked company. Perhaps he liked company because that was a genetic predisposition of his. Perhaps it was a genetic predisposition of his because that sort of genetic predisposition is dominant as most people generally prosper better in groups than as loners. Perhaps that goes back to the animal stage of pre-humans. However one perhaps gets to the point of primitive life forms where living things are just as well off as loners than as part of a group or anyhow to some other point where there is no cause for this but sheer chance. In any event at some point along the line of causes of causes one will surely come to an uncaused cause which far from being some sort of God is probably an element of chance or irrationality. Indeed humans sometimes even attempt - apparently successfully - to rid themselves of causality and make events immediately subject to chance by making them dependent upon tossing a coin or a dice as happens in many games.

So causality therefore doesn't really exist as a comprehensive, or at least comprehensible, all pervading feature of the Universe. Of course there is often a problem of recognising when one has got to an uncaused cause but logic indicates that eventually (if not sooner) any sequence of causality must come to an end.

David Hume also noted that there is a problem in identifying causes and that is even without considering the fact that some things are seemingly caused by a combination of factors and not just one cause. For instance the car crash referred to previously may be caused not just by a semi-drunk driver but also by what led someone else to cross his path. However Hume argued that a regular coincidence or co-appearance of things such as 'smoke' and 'fire' does not in logical terms absolutely necessarily mean that smoke is caused by nor is even necessarily related at all to fire. This I think can in practical terms eventually come to seem unbelievable. However the more significant and indeed insuperable point Hume (and others) has made is that there is no assured continuity of causation.

So the second fundamental problem with causality is that it may not apply universally. For a start it could stop at any moment. To take an analogy, a train may run to a timetable along the rail tracks thousands of times before one time it is suddenly derailed and damaged beyond repair and so no longer runs along the rails to a timetable. Its pattern that continued for so long is destroyed. Much the same actually does happen to every adult human whose heart beats and who breathes air for so many years until he comes to a sudden end to do so no more. So he dies and his regular activities end. Even stars shine for many millions of years until they collapse and die. Indeed planets may orbit a star for millions of years in a regular way until they may be knocked off their orbit by a major collision or even by the gravitational pull of some other passing star. All these events can happen at any time. So at any time a pattern of causality can be broken.

Indeed one may conceive of the whole Universe or at least our part of it at some future time being overwhelmed by a change of conditions from an infusion of irrationality. This hypothetical infusion of irrationality, at least if it grows sufficiently like a tumour might destroy the whole pattern of causation and causality in our area and make our region fundamentally irrational. That would probably make our region unliveable for life forms, or at least for advanced and complex life forms. Indeed other regions of the Universe (or of a hypothecated 'multiverse') may quite possibly be predominantly irrational, existing without a nexus of causality.

So I submit causality perhaps cannot be identified with certainty (as Hume asserted) and, most important, causality cannot be guaranteed to continue for ever. Nor even does causality necessarily exist throughout the Universe. Furthermore it is logically practically certain that at some stage in intellectual proceedings there must be an end to causality or discernible causality and modern science (such as quantum theory) asserts as much. So far from being a constant element of our Universe, causality ultimately, that is after a certain point, disintegrates and vanishes. So after some, albeit useful existence for us, the notion of causality eventually falls into the great, philosophical disintegration and goes into the philosophical black hole.

The end or limitations of the notion of causality unfortunately has dreadful consequences for the scope of human knowledge because our knowledge depends (and I think must depend) so much on the notion of causality. In general human Science and with it human knowledge has advanced as people looked first for 'concomitant events or things' which they reasonably believed to be connected. Those apparent connections form part of our knowledge but people looked from there to the causes of things. It is from deciphering or decoding the apparent causes of things that human science and thereby generally human technology and human knowledge has been able to advance. If this methodology of tracing phenomena down the nexus of causality which has been shown to exist (or at least to exist in most spheres) within our region is or becomes unreliable or non-existent, then the scope for knowledge is severely curbed to say the least.

So the ultimate disintegration of causality which is the main supporting plank for our knowledge, especially our scientific knowledge, has grave consequences for the notion of knowledge. These adverse consequences for the knowability of the Universe that come from the inevitable breakdown of the nexus of causality must apply to any truth-seeker, be he alien, computer or human!

So let us examine what is absolutely knowable and what is not knowable in the light of the qualifications we have had logically to put upon the concept (and nexus) of causality. So far as I can see even in the absence of ultimate certainty about causality two types of knowledge do survive.

As common sense and much scientific enquiry indicates there is at least in our time (as well as during human history) in our region of the Universe some nexus of causality in operation. It is provisional as it can at least potentially change or disappear at any moment and it may not be sustainable as far as ultimate questions are concerned, but it would be foolish to deny that this edifice of causality does exist now. So I would call the knowledge that stems from our local edifice of causality 'provisional knowledge'. It is provisional not because it may all be incorrect or because it may all be inapplicable which are both enormously unlikely notions. It is provisional because it may not (indeed I suspect though I cannot prove it is likely not to) apply at all times nor in all regions of Space nor for all things - in any event it is potentially changeable 'knowledge' .

Yet nevertheless this 'nexus' of causality that clearly exists in our region has enabled people, most notably scientists and technologists to advance our understanding and our prosperity. People can attain greater scientific understanding through further penetrating the codes of causality within that local nexus of causality that does exist now in our region. So I certainly would not despise what has been achieved and what could be achieved for people, say in extending human lifespans, by advancing medical knowledge. The impressive research into decoding complex DNA systems is a good example of this. This is of great practical importance for us humans and is in reality unaffected by any disintegration or black hole of knowledge that may exist further down the philosophical line. So much everyday knowledge which may be of practical use to us can be attained by figuring our way through the nexus of causality that clearly does exist around us. Strictly speaking, I would say all such knowledge is 'provisional knowledge' as in ultimate terms it is. Yet in terms of practical everyday life, as this causal system has at least for the most part actually endured for many millions of years, it is effectively knowledge and very worth attaining. So although the ultimate foundations of most of our knowledge cannot be relied upon, in practical terms the knowledge and knowhow by which we live and increasingly prosper survives pretty much unscathed.

The second element of knowledge that survives the ultimate disintegration of causality is that relatively small part that is not reached by an understanding of the nexus of causality but through an inevitable logic. The most famous instance of this can be found in Rene Descartes' (1596-1650) dictum 'cogito ergo sum' ('I think, therefore I am' or as I prefer 'I think, therefore I exist'). This is founded upon the logical realisation that it is logically absolutely impossible to think (or for that matter to read or write) without existing in some way. The same purely logical approach can be taken to at least much of basic Mathematics and in my opinion to asserting the existence of Space, Time (or at least sequences in time) and colours. So it is possible to understand at least a little bit about the whole ultimate nature of the Universe even from our tiny and in terms of the Universe inconsequential selves, just by the application of inevitable logic that could not be otherwise. I would also add that syllogistic Logic works like that but there can often be difficulties in actually proving the premises one may assert in syllogistic Logic though not the conclusions should the premises be valid. However it is doubtful whether any or much of this logic-derived knowledge is of itself of any or much practical use. This is because when Logic is open to two or usually many more possibilities that may be compatible with it or when the premises themselves are not logically provable, Logic alone cannot yield absolute knowledge that can be guaranteed to be reliable.

Knowledge and Knowability

So in respect of humans or, I submit, any entities (including any possible 'aliens'), the reliability and extent of most of our knowledge is circumscribed by the reliability of the surrounding nexus of causality. Intelligent entities are also of course circumscribed or limited by their intellects or more accurately (to take account of computers, artificial or other intelligences) by the intellects they have access to. Clearly some intelligences, be they aliens or even computers (or artificial intelligences) may be able, possibly through greater cleverness, to advance further than humans can in working within local circumstances (most significantly the local nexus of causality) to achieve more knowledge than lesser intelligences. All this may well embrace sufficient 'knowledge' even if it is provisional for intelligent entities to live well and even perhaps advance exponentially in their ordinary everyday lives. To such knowledge may be added any knowledge that can be gained by purely logical methods.

In conventional philosophical terms I am saying a priori knowledge (which is the minority of knowledge) is unaffected by any breakdown in the nexus of causality. Even an irrational environment cannot for instance make two and two not equal four and cannot make anything 'think' or even 'act' without 'existing' in the first place! However in respect of a posteriori knowledge (empirical knowledge) which is the greater part of what we take to be our knowledge we are dependent upon the existence of a nexus (or nexuses) of causality. No nexus of causality can be guaranteed to carry on for ever and everywhere and in any event in the end it breaks down (on the 'uncaused cause' logic) and is now thought by scientists to break down at quantum level. So a posteriori knowledge is ultimately - though this is of no real consequence at a practical everyday level-merely provisional knowledge. Ultimate knowledge is not attainable or at least not reliably attainable (since it goes beyond the regions of Space and Time we know about or are even ever likely to know about) by 'a posteriori' methods.

There are indeed many questions which are not merely not properly answered now but are in fact uncertain and so unanswerable not just for humans but for all possible intelligences. Such questions include:

> *How big is the Universe (the Universe being 'the totality of existence')?*
> *How far does order in the Universe go back in time?*
> *Will things in the future change fundamentally and perhaps suddenly?*

Will our predominantly rationally arranged (or regularly patterned) area of the Universe in future become unpatterned and predominantly irrational?

How reliable is our knowledge of the Universe?

How far can our understanding of our part of the Universe be reliably extrapolated to the whole Universe?

What is our exact relationship to the Universe as a whole?

Do we unbeknown to us actually merely exist in some more advanced entity's test tube type apparatus?

These and other ultimate questions are unknowable or at least unprovable for us or any entity in the Universe because of what I call Universal Uncertainty.

Universal Uncertainty

The 'Universal Uncertainty' essentially derives from the limitations of immediate (or provisional, or technically a posteriori) knowledge in that we cannot be certain to what extent our observations can properly be extrapolated for ever into Time, Space etc. We cannot even be certain whether our observations are all that accurate (and for instance lack serious distortions), at least beyond the Solar System. Certainly things may change fundamentally and unaccountably at any time or in any region of Space and we have no reliable means of knowing how or indeed whether this might happen. In the end neither we humans nor any entity can be sure that our intellects (or ability to discover ultimate reality) are not limited and as part of the limitations we are unaware of how our intellects are limited. So we must inevitably hit this philosophical barrier to knowledge or at least uncertainty (or philosophical black hole) before we ever reach full ultimate knowledge of how the Universe is constructed. Therefore neither we nor indeed any other intelligence can ultimately be certain of its own relationship to (nor even the extent of) the Universe as a whole which means there are inevitable limits to our or any entity's certain knowledge! That is 'Universal Uncertainty'!

So I am saying in terms of most 'knowledge' when one gets way beyond the level of everyday knowhow that helps us to live, our capacity to know most things eventually disintegrates. Indeed it must eventually disintegrate into a cosmological uncertainty, a universal uncertainty, or universal (or philosophical) black hole.

Incidentally when I write about a philosophical black hole, I do not mean to draw an exact analogy with rather than a close approximation to black holes of Astronomy. It is just the general notion of a black hole that I wish to highlight. In exact terms in the philosophical black hole there is no singularity nor gravitational effect. Unlike its astronomical counterpart, there is no ultimate way out of the philosophical black hole in some guise at the other end. The philosophical black hole is perhaps more like a massive road block travellers may come to and not physically be able to get round or to the other side of. Or perhaps one might say the road just runs out before one gets to one's destination. So I use the term 'philosophical black hole' because it is a stark idea that gives some notion of the situation but it is not intended as an absolutely exact parallel to an astronomical black hole. I use it rather to mean an inherently insuperable barrier absolutely nothing can get past.

So the capacity for most types of knowledge for any human ultimately vanishes and disappears. This is applicable not only to our human knowledge but also to the potential knowledge of any alien or any life form or indeed any existent entity (be it a living thing, a computer, an artificial intelligence or whatnot).

****

So at an ultimate, objective level not only are value judgments such as 'good' or 'beautiful' ultimately unsustainable but so too are more objective notions relating to language, causality and ultimately most types of knowledge. In the end (though not at an everyday level) these kinds of apparent or provisional knowledge all fall into a great universal disintegration of knowledge, or more precisely 'knowability', which in effect is the big philosophical black hole.

Chapter 3: The Philosophy Of Religion And Is There A Purpose To It All?

In this chapter I cross the line from what are generally seen as topics of human knowledge (even if knowledge about human values is rather vague) to what are generally supposed to be just matters of belief even if some religious people think their beliefs are akin to knowledge. I won't repeat too much of what I wrote in my previous book, The Six Ways Of Atheism (which of course I commend) where I set out some logical ways of absolutely disproving the existence of God. However I want to point out this present book sets out a view of the Universe in which God cannot possibly exist and atheism therefore is logically inevitable.

The God Notion

I have been asserting that in the end knowledge ultimately disintegrates into a philosophical black hole through uncertainty about the future and the extent of a rationally ordered cosmos (even apart from possible quantum irregularity and unpredictability). Then for the same reasons as I cite in my Universal Uncertainty Argument in The Six Ways Of Atheism, a monotheistic God (or for that matter significant, enduring polytheistic Gods) is absolutely impossible and atheism is universally inevitable.

My point is that if no entity can legitimately be sure the Universe is not in fact larger than his supposed creation and realm of power, then no entity can have the omniscience necessary to being God. No entity could then be sure there is not some greater entity lurking in realms unknown to him or hidden from him which will ultimately take over his supposed kingdom (as Europeans did to the pre-Columbian American chieftains). Nor could any entity be sure that the present pattern of things or even himself in particular will survive for ever.

Suppose there is indeed beyond a certain point a disintegration and subsequent vanishing in terms of ultimate knowledge that cannot logically be avoided. This is a philosophical logical black hole which prevents anything from being sure about the durability or extent of the Universe. Then an omniscient God just cannot exist. And if any supposed God is not omniscient he cannot be sure there is not some greater, even controlling entity in a realm beyond him and his capacity for knowledge. That must logically apply to any and every 'candidate God', however great his powers and his realm may seem to others and to himself!

Against this it is often fallaciously argued that for all we humans know, some intelligences including God may be able to know things we cannot know - however for all those intelligences (including even any potential God) know there may be yet further things or dimensions that even those intelligences cannot know.

So uncertainty in the end must reign supreme for all things. This is my universal iron 'law of Universal Uncertainty'. Even if some entity seemed like God in all other ways (which seems hardly feasible anyhow in the absence of any all-embracing concept of 'goodness' inherent to the Universe) in the absence of this ultimate knowledge he cannot be sure of his status as God. For instance ultimately there is no way for any entity to be certain it has escaped the problem that no entity can know for certain that it is not somehow limited in its scope and one of its limitations is that it is unable to see its own limitations! So no entity can know that it is omniscient. So no entity can know for sure it is God and so no entity can possibly be God. That is universally true of all otherwise possible Gods. So if one accepts my logical notion that there is a widespread great philosophical disintegration or philosophical black hole underneath the veneer at the core of philosophy, one must necessarily also agree with my atheism.

Afterlife

A similar notion ultimately applies to another topic in the philosophy of religion, afterlife. True, neither the discovery of a philosophical black hole nor indeed the absence of any genuine God does in itself prevent there being some afterlife for humans or other entities. An 'afterlife' could then still occur in the same sort of way that a caterpillar has a kind of afterlife as a butterfly or a foetus has a kind of afterlife as a fully developed human being.

However a philosophical black hole at the core of epistemology does prevent anything being sure that any afterlife is for ever. I myself do not personally think there is any kind of human afterlife, if only because death is a disintegration and breakdown of a person, often as the culmination of a process of degeneration through illness or old age. However I cannot actually disprove there is some afterlife or successor life for humans. It would be very hard to absolutely disprove, however inherently unlikely it may seem, that some practically ethereal spirit within one escapes at death from a corpse and resurrects one's essential being (termed 'soul') in some distant unknown sphere. Yet even if that or something roughly like that were to happen and some people got some afterlife, it cannot be guaranteed that their afterlife would last for ever rather than eventually itself finally die or otherwise come to an end. This is because of everything's inevitable inability to know for certain either the extent or the durability of the 'Universe' (i.e. 'the totality of existence').

So though I cannot logically exclude the possibility (inherently unlikely though it seems to be) of some afterlife or even a succession of afterlifes, what I can exclude is any guarantee (or indeed in reality much likelihood) that any afterlife will endure for all time. This is because nothing here or in any notional afterlife, however advanced or clever it may be, could have any way of knowing that it would not at some time change radically or suddenly disintegrate or otherwise finally end. The philosophical black hole concerning the limits of knowledge logically forces one to that position.

How Did We Come To Exist?

While I am considering the philosophy of religion may I consider briefly the question that supposedly leads so many people (apart from their family background) to a belief in God's existence in the first place. The question is how could intelligent life come to exist without God?

The first answer is it must do so because intelligent, advanced life evidently does exist and God cannot exist. Also, apart even from the reasons for the non-existence of God, using God as the explanation for intelligent life itself entails logical fallacy. In positing God because the existence of intelligent life needs some explanation, one is going logically backwards by positing a yet more intelligent existence (God) which on that criterion would accordingly require even more explanation than us in the first place.

However I think there is in any case another more natural explanation for the existence of intelligent life available to us. This other explanation should be more readily comprehensible to people in our age than it might have been in past ages because in so many ways we are now beginning to notice it occurring in many spheres. I will term it my 'critical mass theory'.

In essence my theory is that when some things reach a critical mass in number, their expansion turns from being merely quantitative to being qualitative as well, which may engender further more rapid and often seemingly exponential development. Sometimes once a critical mass is reached the process even becomes self-generating, as modern insights in various fields are beginning to show. For instance the astronomy of stars according to modern theories seems largely to relate to the thresholds of critical masses at various points causing not merely quantitative but also qualitative changes. Stars are apparently created in the first place when accumulations of matter (or gases) into them reach a critical mass. Then at a further critical mass stars begin to generate their own nuclear fusion (converting hydrogen into helium) and burning off hydrogen until their supply of hydrogen is practically exhausted. Thereafter another critical mass is reached and stars collapse or explode or reach a critical mass to change entirely into a black hole. At each major change in the 'life' of stars the accumulation into a critical mass brings drastic qualitative change. The same appears to be true of computing or even, still speculatively, of artificial intelligence.

While mere abacuses or adding machines do not add very much to human collective knowledge (even if they assist individuals in calculations), the calculations many computers are now capable of do. Nowadays computers can do calculations that are so complicated (more complicated even than practically any human individually is capable of completing) that they may not merely speed up the process of knowing. They may also reveal or indicate new truths that extend our knowledge or provide the groundwork for technological improvements. At some point artificial intelligences might reach that critical mass by which they do not merely reflect our human intelligences but may extend it or even one day replicate themselves.

Indeed I say more generally when an entity, be it microbe or artificial intelligence, has reached a point when it can reproduce its species and does so it has reached a critical mass that is not merely quantitative but also qualitative in its nature. In this vein I suggest the origin and development of advanced life on Earth and in the Universe is best explained not by a theory of some omnipotent, eternal, creating God making it or setting its development in motion. Rather a better explanation is that some elements of matter in the Universe develop (much as stars do) into a critical mass and when they get to that critical mass sometimes they change not merely quantitatively but also qualitatively. This may - and I think does - bring into existence some previously unknown development, be it reproduction or the genesis of intelligent life or whatever. But as with the clumping together of matter to form stars, neither the process nor the elements involved need be eternal, omnipotent, omniscient, conscious nor 'good'. Indeed they generally are not these things. Just as clumps of matter (or gases) that form stars are not divine, neither I say is our Universe or even the Universe's ultimate creator or creative process divine.

Purpose

Nor need there be, indeed I say nor can there be, any real or ultimate purpose to our (or even any alien's) existence.

To repeat briefly what I stated in my book, The Six Ways Of Atheism, in the first place as far as conscious humans (or indeed any advanced life forms) are concerned, there could hardly be a real purpose to life if those living life do not know what it is. There cannot be much of a real purpose in practice if we are in ignorance of it and therefore are unable to live consciously in accordance with it. There certainly is no consensus among people now (nor indeed at any historical time) about what the purpose of either life or the Universe is.

However there is a second and even more compelling reason why our life, indeed all life, all existence is without genuine purpose and that is because there inherently cannot be any ultimate purpose to life or the Universe. If one asks what is the purpose of any life, one starts off on a regression that eventually leads nowhere, that ultimately can only lead nowhere.

Suppose one asks, to take an awkward example, what is the purpose of a cow named Daisy in a field? The most accurate answer would seem to be, if there is a purpose, it is to provide food for humans though geneticists might say it is to continue the line of cattle by producing calves. That just goes to show that the notion of purpose can usually be considered in many different ways anyhow. But to proceed nevertheless, what is the purpose of feeding humans? Well, feeding humans promotes the wellbeing of humans. This brings us onto the question of what is the purpose of humans, especially as mankind will eventually become extinct? Whatever answer one then gives one can continually thereafter, even apart from questioning whether any proffered purpose is actually accurate, then ask what is the purpose of that? Eventually one may inaccurately and wrongly go into a nonsensical and logically wrong circularity of argument (for instance claiming, as many mistakenly do, that the purpose of life is 'to worship God' and the purpose of worshipping God is 'to fulfil one's purpose in life'). Or else one may accurately get to the point where no further or no underlying purpose to any supposed purpose that one posits can legitimately be found. So ultimately there is no underlying purpose to the Universe which its vagaries and apparent needless hardships would indicate in the very first place anyhow!

This should be even more evident because in general 'change' is necessary to our living and indeed to any life. Probably one of the essential characteristics or qualities in life, any life, is that of being an agent of change, if only to obtain the nutrition or energy necessary for keeping oneself alive. Yet change is generally to the benefit of some things (such as humans when they eat fish or even rice) but at the expense of other things (the fish or rice grains which were being devoured and done away with in those instances!). We may indeed in practice yet illogically value some things (naturally ourselves) as of more importance than other things but as I've stated before values are ultimately unreal and artificial. So just as there is (as I previously argued) no inherent value to one thing rather than another thing existing, there is no inherent universal purpose to the changes that make some things rather than others exist. Without some ultimate 'value' to anything there may at most be mechanisms for change and also sequences of changes but there cannot be any ultimate universal purpose of any inherent value. So in effect there can be no ultimate purpose to anything that exists.

****

So, to summarise, the topics within the philosophy of religion, God, afterlife and 'ultimate purpose' would not normally be considered part of human knowledge as such, rather than part of human beliefs. Nevertheless 'the great disintegration' in knowledge and philosophy does show that in absolute terms none of these, God, any permanent afterlife, nor 'ultimate purpose' can ultimately be confirmed or identified. However we can use a rather clever logical argument to show that if it cannot be identified (as self identification is absolutely necessary to a potential monotheistic God and at least very desirable in terms of purpose) God and maybe ultimate purpose cannot exist. Furthermore in the case of any potential afterlife one could never legitimately allay any gnawing uncertainty over whether it may all anyhow end.

So a clever use and understanding of the consequences of the inevitable black hole of knowledge or philosophy does when universalised (as can legitimately be done) yield us some actual absolute knowledge.

At least we may thereby know that the existence of a monotheistic God is logically unviable and therefore impossible. We may also know that the inevitable limitations besetting our knowledge of the Universe are indeed universal and insuperable for all forms of life (or even existence, including artificial intelligences) that care to look diligently and accurately into these matters.

Chapter 4: Is This 'Philosophical Black Hole' Dependent Upon Logic?

Now I do acknowledge that 'the great disintegration' I speak of is discovered by the use of Logic (some may say 'human logic'). People might then claim that if this is where 'Logic' leads us, it doesn't show that there is ultimately a 'great disintegration' but alternatively that Logic is either ultimately wrong or anyhow limited in its applicability. That is a perfectly reasonable, indeed logical, point to consider and a point that really does need answering.

Just One Universal Logic

Let me first deal with a supposed distinction beloved by some theologians (and even perhaps by some speculative scientists) between 'Logic' and mere 'human logic'. 'Human logic' is supposedly distinct from some supposed divine or perhaps even alien Logic which (conveniently) we know nothing about, except that some people merely claim that it must exist! I emphatically reject any distinction between 'Logic', 'human logic' or any other valid kind of Logic. I say there can only be one valid form of Logic which is a universal Logic (although I do of course acknowledge that we humans probably do not as yet know everything it is logically possible to know within this one universal system of Logic). Statements or propositions are either 'logically correct' or 'logically wrong' or indeed most frequently 'logically indeterminable and so not determinable by logic alone'.

There is not and cannot be any system of logic where 'cogito ergo sum' ('I think therefore I exist') does not apply. There can be no legitimate system of logic where a mortal entity can be sure of identifying correctly an immortal entity because any mortal entity has not lived and will not live long enough to have any way of being sure there will be no, even irrational change.

Furthermore the notion of other Universes or a 'multiverse' does not alter that universally applicable logic. I personally reject the notion of 'multiverse' anyhow because I define the Universe as 'the totality of existence'. Furthermore I am very sceptical about there being countless entirely separate 'Universes' in a multiverse without some seepage from one Universe to another Universe. So I don't like the multiverse theory just as I don't like Leibniz' theory of countless entirely separated 'windowless monads'.

Anyhow, though there may well be other regions of the Universe (or other cosmoses) that operate under different physical systems and different scientific 'laws' to ours, there can be no other system of Logic. It is not good enough to assert there are or may be other systems of logic and then say we do not or cannot understand them. That is not good enough because there is a basic universal logic to 'I think, therefore I exist'. Under any system it is universally impossible to think without existing! There is also a basic universal truth to the concepts that 'mortals cannot be certain of correctly identifying immortal entities (as mortals do not live long enough to do so)' or even 'patterns within the Universe are liable to change from time to time unbeknown to living entities'. Such statements are universally true and cannot be other than universally true. Furthermore what is not universally true or universally applicable, though it might well be a feature of the Universe, is not and cannot be determinable by Logic alone nor by the Logic of the Universe.

What If I Am Wrong About Logic?

So when I assert that my discovery of a 'great disintegration' or 'philosophical black hole' is the inexorable result of correct logical analysis, I say it must be true and cannot be otherwise. But what, you may ask, if I am wrong about Logic and either Logic does not ultimately apply at all in the Universe or there are unbeknown to us other or alternative logical systems?

Though I emphatically reject those notions that are contrary to the Logic of the Universe, such hypotheses could not eradicate 'the great disintegration' or 'philosophical black hole' so far as we or other intelligences are concerned. Such notions would merely hasten the inevitable arrival of the 'great disintegration of knowledge' which is 'the philosophical black hole'.

If hypothetically we cannot be sure even of our logic, then there is nothing at all we can be certain of. Then not only would our scientific and everyday empirical knowledge be merely provisional (until we know better or experience things differently) as it is, but so too would be the remainder of the sphere of possible knowledge, a priori knowledge. Then a priori knowledge derived from Logic would also fall into this great disintegration, this philosophical black hole. So if we cannot be certain of the correctness of our logic, then we cannot be certain of anything at all. Then the ancient Greek, Gorgias of Leontini (c490BC-385BC) who claimed 'nothing can be known and we cannot know anything' would indeed be correct and Descartes and I would be wrong.

Yet what would then be clear even in an irrational world (or even in a world operating through some supposed 'logic' which we do not or cannot understand) is that there is a 'great disintegration of all our conceivable knowledge' which is a philosophical black hole. Then that 'great disintegration of knowledge' (or 'philosophical black hole') would be even more comprehensive, indeed totally comprehensive, than I am myself willing to acknowledge. The 'philosophical black hole' might also be encountered even more quickly once one has pierced the veneer of our provisional everyday knowledge. Indeed we in practice live by the reasonable assumption (though not proof) that what has occurred several times is likely to recur more times and what has occurred very many times is likely (though not certain) to occur many more times. Without those assumptions upon which everyday life is largely based, the 'philosophical black hole' would in practice be reached very much more quickly!

****

So what I am saying is that there is a 'great disintegration' or philosophical black hole that one logically must reach when one contemplates most 'ultimate' or underlying or fundamental questions upon logical analysis. However even if 'logic' and such 'logical analysis' were not correct or not available to us, then one would inevitably still get to this same 'great disintegration' of ultimate knowledge and values but that 'great disintegration' would be even more comprehensive. Instead of eventually mainly swallowing up most 'ultimate' knowledge, it might swallow up practically all human knowledge and do so even more quickly than the 'philosophical black hole' I myself envisage. Either way the massive philosophical black hole or 'great disintegration of knowledge' which I have here demonstrated necessarily applies to humans and all intelligent entities must inevitably exist and ultimately be integral to universal existence. It must apply from the vantage point or perspective of any existent entity (that is capable of understanding it) and limit our or any entity's possible knowledge.

Part II - Philosophy From An Alien's Perspective

Chapter 5: The Humancentric Parts Of Philosophy

We, that is myself and my readers are all humans and we cannot get away from that. As humans we naturally have human prejudices and human perspectives. However we can – even if no great philosopher in the past bothered to do so - examine our views and our approaches carefully to separate out what in philosophy is merely humancentric from what is, at least potentially, universal. To help us do so we can and probably should view the whole of philosophy from the viewpoint or perspective of some extraterrestrial alien or even some 'artificial intelligence'.

Mere Human Opinions

As we have seen what we term 'values' and 'aesthetics' are not universally ingrained into the Universe but only make much sense to us from a human perspective.

Values may at least in part be utilitarian in nature in that they may help human societies to prosper but they are certainly humancentric. Just as previously the survival of dinosaurs was good for dinosaurs but not for mammals who superseded them as the dominant animals on Earth, human survival is good for humans and their advancement. However it is not necessarily good for those other life forms that might otherwise be more dominant on Earth.

Furthermore to be of much use human values have to correlate not with what may be abstractly desirable but with human nature. For instance humans tend to be competitive in their nature and do best under competitive circumstances. So it is not useful nor sensible for humans to attach (as some philosophers - e.g. Stoics - have) an overriding value to 'serenity' or even 'serenity' between humans. However that is not to say that 'serenity' might not be a sensible priority for aliens or indeed other animals (such as perhaps pack animals like dogs) who are not so reliant upon individual competitiveness. They may for instance best achieve their objectives or greatest strength by altruistic mutual cooperation. 'Serenity' could also be useful to those whose greatest weakness may be a predisposition to panic. There is nothing universal about this - rather each life form or intelligence does best with 'values' that best match and correspond with its own nature.

This is even more evidently true of 'aesthetics' where each entity, human, animal or alien, has aesthetic notions arising from its own nature rather than from any universal truth. For instance it is of no genetic use for a man to fall in love with a female pig or a male pig to find human women rather than female pigs beautiful or arousing - and so this generally does not happen. Humans have human based notions of beauty and pigs doubtless have pig based notions of beauty. I suppose alien extra-terrestrials, if they have any aesthetic notions each have their own brand of alien based notions of aesthetics. There is nothing universal in aesthetics. Aesthetics are in general species based and indeed within a very general species spectrum, aesthetics are often individually based on individuals.

The same pretty well applies to languages as is demonstrated by the multiplicity of human languages. If advanced aliens exist, the reasonable assumption is that they too would have their own language or at any rate their own mode of communication between themselves. Quite sensibly practically nobody expects aliens to communicate between themselves in any human language. It is also true that all human languages have their imprecisions, ambiguities, gaps and weaknesses and it is possible that that is true of all languages in the Universe though it might not be. Some alien languages and even more so languages among artificial intelligences might be very precise and exact and unambiguous and even fairly comprehensive unlike human languages. This could be especially so if (to some extent like Esperanto) the language was deliberately developed and adopted, unlike human languages, to be or become a perfect medium for communication. Such a carefully created language might potentially reduce or even eliminate the philosophical problems highlighted in the human philosophy of language, problems that arise largely because of imprecisions in our linguistic communication. Certainly a more carefully constructed and developed language should make it clear that language exists for the expression of thoughts or instruction and is not the basis via its linguistic deficiencies for insights into the nature of reality, as too many philosophers have supposed.

An alien visitor might well be surprised by the varying human notions of God which evidently demonstrate that human minds invent Gods rather than that any God created humans. Obviously it is not impossible that an alien might have its own notion of God. Its God might have sent down some Messiah alien of its own race to tell his ancestors of the possible salvation for aliens only available through following the precepts of that alien Messiah formulated through his direct revelations from his alien God! However when this alien (with or without belief in his own alien Messiah) comes to Earth he could be much amused by how different people follow, often to the point of death, contradictory religions. There is Christianity with its personal God, Islam with its impersonal God and Hinduism with its multiplicity of Gods, many of which are on view in Hindu temples or even in local Hindu shrines.

'Gods' on Earth are very evidently not manifestations of any universal truth but are humancentric, indeed mere ancient inventions of the societies that originally worshipped them! Human notions of afterlife are just as diverse and variable and are just as clearly humancentric notions. They are the myths of human societies rather than the reflexions of any universal truths.

To some extent even our Science is distorted by humancentricity because apart from its being centred on the human environment in and around Earth its questions are set by humans and its research efforts are directed by humans. Then its research findings are interpreted by humans who have in their minds their own human predispositions and human prejudices.

It is worth bearing in mind that if Science was conducted by aliens, it would be centred on the environment of their 'home territory' in their part of the Universe and its questions would be set by those aliens. The research would then be devised by these aliens and it would be interpreted from the perspective of their alien predispositions and alien prejudices.

Of course (human) scientists would generally say they are aiming at something more objective than that. However the history of Science shows that humans, even supposedly objective scientists, have found it peculiarly hard not to interpret phenomena to accord with their natural predispositions and indeed prejudices. I.Q. (human intelligence) research has been a particular case in point. Another example is that though no biologist has any difficulty in agreeing that women do on average live significantly longer than men, most are quite incapable no matter how much data may indicate it of acknowledging publicly that men are better than women in some very crucial matters. Men are much more likely and able to make pioneering discoveries (such as in computing) or to become billionaires or chess champions than women are.

Though in theory scientists claim to be objective or aim for objectivity, especially in their analysis of their own results, very often this is not achieved because they are too concerned to make their science accord with their preconceived notions or prejudices. Some aliens may bring similar shortcomings to their scientific endeavours though some may not. I suspect computers or artificial intelligences could well do better in scientific endeavours. So although in theory Science should be objective and universal (or at least provisionally applicable in our region of the Universe), our science is all too often infected and corrupted by humancentric prejudices. Classic examples include the longheld human insistence that the Sun revolves around the Earth as the centre of the Universe and that mankind is apart from rather than evolved from other animals! I hope human scientific endeavours could be more objective in the future and not tainted by human prejudices but I would not guarantee it.

The Mind/Body Relationship

Turning to another branch of philosophy, philosophers have long been intrigued by the relationship between the human mind (or sometimes a 'human soul') and the human body which is surely a very humancentric topic in philosophy. In fact I say it really is or should be a scientific or physiological question rather than a philosophical question. If we were television sets or computers or even artificial intelligences such a question just wouldn't be puzzling. That is because we would then come into (and out of) existence or rather operation when all our essential component parts are assembled in a workable way. Obviously things seem somewhat more complicated in the case of human beings (or animals) but the principle may be just the same.

I suspect we work or operate through the combination of our vital parts operating in tandem but even if that were not quite so, there is no necessary fundamental division between the human body and 'the human spirit'.

For instance if people have a highish physical temperature and they become delirious their minds tend to become delusional - so then human minds and bodies work in tandem and in association. It is probably humancentric romanticism that draws a qualitative division between visible human bodies and invisible human minds. There probably is no real or qualitative division and most probably (contrary to romantic or wishful notions) when human bodies die, so too do human minds.

In any event the relationship between human minds and human bodies is not properly a speculative matter for philosophy. It being an empirical matter there is and probably can be no compelling logic about the matter and so it is a proper matter for scientific physiological enquiry.

I suppose the mind/body question landed with philosophy because it is a distinction that appears to have struck the consciousness of human beings before the advent of significant human science. It has probably been maintained in philosophy because mystics in just about all religions (indeed the mainstream of most religions from ancient times such as in the ancient Egyptian religion right up to modern times) have seen such a distinction. In many religions such as Buddhism that distinction remains pretty well paramount to the religion. The distinction between a body that very evidently dies and decays and a spirit they hope does not is critical to making many religions, or indeed many human fantasies or wishes, possible. Yet that is not to say it is correct rather than mere wishful human imaginings or that it should be a matter for philosophy or that scientific explanation for this hypothesised dichotomy is impossible.

I rather think proper scientific explanation is not merely possible but will come in the not too distant future. In any event philosophising about this problem is mere human speculation and will get us nowhere whereas scientific enquiry is the only hope, and I think a good hope of solving this apparent problem. Such questions are after all neither matters soluble by logic alone (a priori) nor are questions of 'should' or 'ought' (such as ethics). Therefore mind/body relationship questions do not properly fall within the realm of Philosophy but are exclusively matters for Science. So an intelligent alien would very likely understand our and his own inner workings or at least that it is just a matter for enquiring scientifically into. He might be amused that humans consider the relationship between their minds and their bodies to be a matter for religion or philosophy rather than for physiological science!

Human Psychology

Another facet of human intellectual behaviour which might well amuse an intelligent alien is the human trait of people somehow coming to believe what they seem psychologically to want to believe in. This applies almost irrespective of evidence and certainly irrespective of Logic. It has now been demonstrated by scientists that many humans can and do subconsciously create false memories, that is a memory of and a sincere belief in the occurrence of events that never actually happened in their lives. Similarly most people seem to have a great capacity after some prompting to adopt false and illogical beliefs. So humans seem to have a natural predisposition to believe that such things as 'good' or 'beauty' or 'god' really exist. People also tend to believe that everything is at least potentially knowable.

True, people may cite every scrap of poor or even irrelevant evidence for their beliefs, such as specific events or whatever. Yet it could surely amuse an alien that because people don't know how ultimately the world came to exist, they somehow suppose that is a valid way to know that God must have created it - knowledge deriving from ignorance!

It may be that human groups and societies benefit from and maintain better cohesion because of people's psychological innate tendency to believe in God or goodness or beauty.

Certainly most people seem instinctively predisposed to believe in supernatural superstitions and even more so in absolute 'good' and 'bad'. Richard Dawkins (born 1941) thinks that belief in God is like a virus acting upon and weakening, as viruses do, many human brains. However I observe evidence that an irrational human belief in the objectively non-existent notion of goodness is even more widespread and fundamental to humans. Indeed the accepted and normal notion of people having 'a conscience' shows how deeply ingrained belief in 'good' and 'bad', moral 'right' and 'wrong' is in humans and in human society. So I think these irrational (or at any rate incorrect) beliefs in supernatural superstitions, goodness and indeed beauty are not fundamentally viruses, but a normal, perhaps beneficial, yet systemic faulty setting (in terms of raw intelligence) of human minds.

People clearly originally evolved as family or clan animals. So one should appreciate that important though harnessing the brainpower of outstanding individuals has now become to human history, human development and modern human society, people are not primarily 'brain' or 'intelligence' 'animals' but group or social animals. The benefits to a group (such as in the promotion of the group's wellbeing through group cohesion and acceptable social behaviour) that a natural belief in goodness and perhaps to a lesser extent in a common God (or gods) confer might naturally outweigh any tendency to maximise sheer human brainpower. Modern computers or artificial intelligences might be designed as intelligence, even intelligence maximising, machines. Perhaps some alien living entities in outer Space have evolved or even designed themselves to maximise intelligence. Human beings most certainly are not and never have been designed primarily to maximise intelligence. Human instincts in the overwhelming majority of humans seem focused upon maintaining good psychological morale and individual human comforts and indeed just life within human extended families and originally small human societies. Thus comes beliefs in 'God' (or Gods) and 'goodness' and also, incidentally, natural human tendencies towards xenophobia, racism and hostility to deviation from society's norms, be it via physical differences from other humans or mental dissent.

It takes a great deal to change these natural human predispositions. Yet what may change these human predispositions is if some of the leading acknowledged experts in a society begin to accept new insights and so then deviate either from their previous opinion, or at any rate from the opinions of the previous generation of expert opinion. This is because many people being essentially sheepish group animals (who follow the multitude or leading opinion) don't wish to deviate from a contemporary consensus of accepted leading opinion! It can however become quite a battle when most expert opinion conflicts with psychologically comfortable or comforting opinion on an emotive subject, as is sometimes now the case. Do people want conformity or psychological comfort more - that is quite a question! Where comfortable, convenient opinions and conformity match for humans, that becomes an overwhelming force of opinion, however irrational the opinion may actually be in logical terms. If eventually psychologically comfortable opinions and conformity diverge (because of widely acknowledged expert opinion) over emotive subjects, that can become a great conflict of ideas!

So society based instincts or values within almost all humans are often hindrances to the pursuit of truth. We should become aware of this human predisposition to favour and then as a consequence bend scraps of alleged evidence towards establishing false constructs of the human mind. This common and generally subconscious human behaviour may be a psychological comfort but it is a philosophical and intellectual weakness for humans.

Ethics and Politics

However what is undoubtedly a matter in which philosophers can take a legitimate interest are ethics and politics wherein there are no absolutely correct or incorrect views but only more or less appropriate views. These are questions of 'ought' rather than scientific (or logical) questions of 'is' and therefore are appropriate to philosophy. That said they are very much concerned with human beings and so what is appropriate to human beings and human nature is not necessarily appropriate to aliens or other intelligent entities.

I have already skirted around 'ethics' when I considered the notions of 'values' and 'goodness'. Many people think values such as 'good' are central to ethics. Yet that is only one, albeit the dominant view of ethics. However if 'good' did not exist in absolute terms we, as humans, would still have to establish a 'modus vivendi' ('a way of living'), appropriate to humans and human society.

Indeed there are ways not based on any absolute concept of goodness that could achieve a viable ethical system for society. There is Jeremy Bentham's (1748-1832) notion of 'the greatest happiness of the greatest number'. Although I do not entirely agree with it, at least happiness does exist from the human perspective and is very likely potentially measurable. So it is a possible approach. Or one could go for another version of 'pragmatism' by which human ethics would not be constructed on mythical (when examined) metaphysical concepts such as 'goodness' but upon what is most compatible with the welfare or prosperity of human society in general. This is very humancentric but it is in principle sensible as a philosophy though of course there are issues within it such as the degree to which one should encourage individualism at the expense of collectivism or vice versa that are as yet far from clear. However what can be said is that the most appropriate pragmatic systems of ethics for alien entities are likely to work out very differently in practice from what is most appropriate for humans. So not only pragmatism but ethics in general are not based on universal truths but are essentially creature (be they humans or aliens) centred. The same must surely apply to politics and political philosophy.

Politics - at least human politics - is in general and in philosophy more complicated and more complex than ethics. For instance leadership and governance does not feature much in ethics but is a fundamental theme in political philosophy. Unlike what tends to be universalist ethical theories, governance and governance theories tend to be grounded in or at least speculated about in relation to actual human experience.

Even within a system or society where one person rules (and of course there can be systems of joint, collective or even democratic leadership) that person may be selected for different reasons. It may for instance be his popularity, his exemplary strength, his knowledge or his family relationship to the previous leader. It is hard to develop and justify a universalist political theory that pronounces that one of these qualities (or some specific combination of these qualities) should win out in the selection of a society's leader or leadership. Much, I suggest, would depend on the characters and circumstances of the individuals that comprise that society, be it a human, an animal or an alien society. For instance elephant groups tend to prize knowhow while lions prefer dominant strength and chimpanzees tend to go for a combination of strength and popularity. Humans are more variable in what they go for. Indeed among human societies, especially advanced human societies, the qualities they go for in choosing a leader are quite liable to change from time to time. It is hard to argue that any of these systems holds any inherent universal truth rather than it is and should be a matter of each according to his taste and circumstances which is pragmatic.

The same applies to any society or group of aliens or extra-terrestrials: the way they are organised or governed is not to be derived from universalist laws but rather from their own individual natures, propensities and circumstances. This is also true of other parts of political philosophy such as the distribution of wealth (hardly a great philosophical question in nomadic hunter-gatherer societies or groups) or honour or even freedom. So if not all, then at least most of political philosophy is necessarily humancentric rather than universal, based therefore on a kind of pragmatism rather than universalism.

The same of course applies to that part of essentially political philosophy (or perhaps more accurately political prejudice!) now called 'feminism'. For a start aliens might not have two genders but one or otherwise multiple genders. Even if there were two genders the physical and other relationships between them might be (as to an extent they do vary between human societies) more or less equal than in most human societies.

Anyhow, most if not all groups of entities do require or at least in practice have some sort of political philosophy. That is practically unavoidable, if only because the relationship between an individual and other individuals even within a group, let alone a group's relationship with other similar and dissimilar groups is essentially a part of political philosophy. However an alien would rightly find that human political philosophy and political practices stem from the existence of human groups and from living on Earth, not from any universal truth. Furthermore an intelligent alien would probably see that in its alien society its political practices and philosophy would really relate primarily to its own alien society. Indeed what is practised or appropriate for even other types of alien (or even artificial intelligence) society might be very different. So political philosophy is primarily without absolute truth but is mainly a pragmatic investigation into what is politically most appropriate to the nature of the individuals and to the circumstances that pertain to particular societies.

****

So it is safe to conclude that most human philosophy has in reality nothing to do with finding some universalist absolute truths but is essentially humancentric. So if such philosophy were engaged in by Martians it would be Martian-centric, if engaged in by Alpha-Centaurians it would be Alpha-Centaurian centric and if it was engaged in by other aliens it would be those other alien-centric. This applies to the ethics, aesthetics and politics in philosophy as well as to values and linguistic philosophy. However there is another part of Philosophy, the search for fundamental truths and the nature of the Universe which is absolute and universal. In that part of Philosophy extra-terrestrial aliens, if they philosophised, even from their very different locations and circumstances in

Space, would necessarily be asking the same fundamental
questions as we do. I now turn to this.

Chapter 6: The Universal Part Of Philosophy

It is not without reason that originally Science was called 'natural philosophy'. Philosophy was at one time all embracing. It concerned questions which we would nowadays term as 'scientific' as well as other questions we would now term as moral or political or metaphysical (such as why we exist or what is the nature of the Universe?).

Admittedly I do not believe all the boundaries in this division of the once all-embracing term 'philosophy' have been properly drawn. I have argued that the relationship between mind and body is properly a scientific rather than a modern philosophical (or metaphysical) question. In essence the proper division between scientific and philosophical questions should be the division between those factual questions that are at least hypothetically determinable by scientific experiment and research and those which are not. Those which are not can be divided into factual existential questions (which are broadly speaking 'metaphysical') and those which concern our values or attitudes (which are broadly speaking 'ethical'). Ethical questions are for us essentially humancentric, grounded in our natures, environment and circumstances as people. Far from being of universal applicability they would probably be responded to differently in respect of other animals or in respect of aliens in outer space. By contrast let me elaborate on my view that 'metaphysical questions' even if they are mostly ultimately unanswerable (because of a great disintegration of knowledge or 'philosophical black hole') are universally applicable. They are just as relevant, cogent and potentially mystifying for any aliens as they are for human beings.

Metaphysical Questions

People naturally ask and have long asked, how did we and things come into existence in the first place? Probably people have been spurred on to ask that question because they see some regular, consistent nexus of causality (for instance boiling water causes steam) at work in the world. People have then extrapolated from that (I think wrongly) to assuming that everything, including our existence and the Universe as a whole must have some cause. People also ask questions like what is the extent in time or Space of the Universe and is there a God and what is truth and how ultimately can we learn the real truth? These are questions that aliens, indeed all life forms (Martians or Alpha-Centaurians or anything) may legitimately ask, however technologically advanced they are.

Many aliens may have more scientific knowledge than us which could be very useful to them (as our science is to us) but it is all ultimately provisional knowledge and liable to change, decay and destruction. This is analogous to a train that runs regularly and usefully along tracks for a very long time but is ultimately liable to change, decay and destruction. However the question what is the real truth that lies behind all these changing and potentially variable features of the Universe is in essence a universal question, equally pertinent to all entities everywhere.

Unfortunately we reach an inevitable philosophical disintegration of knowledge or a philosophical black hole before we get to most ultimate answers. So most such questions are equally insoluble (except in a few cases such as there can be no God which is equally soluble) to all entities throughout the Universe. The problem that is the crux of this philosophical black hole is that there appear to be no logically clear answers and anyhow no universal answers inherent in the Universe. There are (at most) just different viewpoints from different places or different situations in the Universe. In any case practically everything is liable to change and thus uncertainty. So at the end of such enquiries there is universal uncertainty.

This universal uncertainty is inevitable because we and all entities appear to be mortal in time and limited to a region of Space. At the very least no entity (even some otherwise Godlike entity which is the greatest possible entity) can have any sure way of knowing that it is not mortal and is not merely limited to some small (indeed relatively infinitesimal) region of Space. Any entity, however sophisticated it may appear, may for all it or we know be merely the equivalent to some test tube 'culture experiment' (possibly even within a test tube 'culture experiment') that is incapable of even seeing to the boundary of its test tube.

Yes, within ultimate questions even from our possibly minimal existence we can know for certain that as we apparently exist in the Universe there must be a Universe. If we exist (as we must do to even contemplate such questions) we must exist within the totality of existence, the Universe which must therefore exist. We can also be certain that as there are apparent sequences within our lives that Time must also inevitably exist in some way. The same can certainly be said of Space (through differentiations in Space) and probably colour as well. Yet this seems merely to amount to identifying a few necessarily existent components of the Universe, not to a thorough nor even satisfactory understanding of the Universe as a whole. However as this is logically based knowledge, this is also knowledge that any alien able to do Logic can gain independently of us through its own existence.

Yet these little points of ultimate knowledge arise from a compelling universal logic, not from scientific enquiry. So no alien, however technologically advanced it is, may be able to go further in its ultimate understanding of the Universe. At any rate no alien can possibly overcome the inevitable barriers to such universal knowledge, the inability to be absolutely sure of its own relationship both in Time and Space to the Universe as a whole. This is because there is no possible, reliable, certain method of acquiring the knowledge to become legitimately absolutely sure of this. In the last resort no entity can know for certain that it is not limited in its scope and one of its limitations is that it is unable to see its own limitations.

This is an essentially epistemological problem that is insuperable for all humans, all aliens and indeed all intelligences. So it forms one part of the universal 'philosophical black hole' that exists. Another part of this 'philosophical black hole' is what swallows up any core basis for 'values', aesthetics and indeed ethics. This ensures an inability for any entity within any pattern of the Universe (that is any entity) to legitimately endorse the worth of one type of pattern rather than another type of pattern within the Universe. There is no discoverable or logically possible inherent validation of the worth of one pattern of existence rather than any other pattern of existence within the Universe. One cannot legitimately objectively validate the inherent worth of some things rather than other things existing and forming a part of the pattern of the Universe. A third part of this 'philosophical black hole' arises for us, for instance in linguistic philosophy, from our own human inability to be precise-though this part of the philosophical black hole may possibly not apply to some aliens.

However in general a 'philosophical black hole' or 'great disintegration in knowledge' must apply universally to all aliens as well as to us whether they care about it or not. Beyond even conceivable doubt it applies in relation to epistemology through a general impossibility of being sure oneself or indeed any conscious entity is not merely a temporary phenomenon within a perhaps rather untypical and unrepresentative location in Space. It (the philosophical black hole) also exists because of an ultimately general impossibility of underpinning through the fabric of the Universe any value judgments we or any aliens may make or actually adopt.

Problems that are logically impossible to overcome are logically impossible not only for us humans but also likewise for any aliens or even any artificial intelligences to overcome. They are just logically impossible and every entity within the Universe (i.e. within 'the totality of existence') must if it cares to analyse it properly be in exactly the same situation about that. Such ultimate 'universal uncertainty' in and concerning the Universe just cannot be overcome by anything.

CONCLUSION

This book is short but it does break new ground in philosophy and sets out a radically different view to that of any of the great philosophers. Although I encompass some subsidiary points (such as arguing that human minds have a natural predisposition to falsely invent and then believe in concepts they like such as goodness or god), I argue for two major theses.

The first thesis is that Philosophy should be examined to see what within it is humancentric and what is truly universal. I suggest the best way of doing this is by looking down on Philosophy from the hypothetical viewpoint of an extra-terrestrial alien. From there it should become clear that much human philosophy is developed and considered (usually this is unnoticed by the people doing philosophy) from a purely human viewpoint primarily to accommodate human societies and human predispositions. This is true for instance of ethics, political philosophy, linguistics, aesthetics and notions of 'good' and 'bad' and values. An alien existing in different circumstances in a different region of the Universe in a different type of society among different natured creatures would be very likely to have very different views on these philosophical questions.

However there are other topics in Philosophy that look beyond purely human society or any purely alien society to questions about the fundamental nature of the Universe. Some such questions are why the Universe exists, how the Universe could have come to exist and whether the Universe can have purpose infused within it or be a product of God. There are also questions about the nature of Truth and indeed the nature of Logic that are truly universal and are as applicable to any alien as much as they are to humans. Such questions do not in essence differ between humans and aliens or indeed between humans and any entity in the Universe wherever they are or however they exist.

My second thesis is that there is a philosophical black hole at the central core of most philosophy. In terms of 'value questions' we are caught in the black hole that there logically can be no ultimate values. In terms of universal questions of fact and the ultimate relationship of any entity to its environment as a whole we are necessarily caught in the black hole of 'universal uncertainty'. Nothing can escape from that.

True, we or aliens or other entities may to a considerable extent work along 'a nexus of causality' (and regularity) that we notice in the area around us to achieve in our time and in our area much technological advancement and comfort. However all this 'knowledge' is ultimately only 'provisional knowledge' that is ultimately subject to change (just as any train is subject to derailment) at any time. Indeed there may conceivably be different 'nexuses of causality' in operation in different regions of the Universe. Actually it would be very hard, if not impossible, for any advanced life to survive without some nexus of causality system around it. Otherwise the unpredictability of things would probably then be just too difficult for living things to cope with. However when one looks beyond such nexuses of causality to the real and permanent nature of things (akin to the hardware of the Universe rather than just the software patterns within the Universe to use computing terms) one encounters insuperable problems.

Both we and anyone or anything can know for certain very little beyond that a few fundamental elements (such as different material-type-existences such as ourselves, Time and Space) must actually exist in the Universe. As we are limited in time and limited spatially (or at the very least in the case of every conscious entity it can have no way of being absolutely sure that it is not so limited) for the most part neither we nor anything else can be certain about the absolute nature of things. Thus beyond our provisional knowledge about our own and probably local nexus of causality (which our intellects may partly penetrate) we, as would any intelligence, encounter a great philosophical black hole of either uncertainty or non-answers (in the case of values) which we cannot avoid.

So my second thesis is that at the core of most philosophical questions we come to a great disintegration of knowledge and a great philosophical intellectual black hole of either non-answers or universal uncertainty. This is an intellectual black hole which neither we nor any entity throughout the Universe can possibly escape from which marks the end of possible knowledge for us or anything.

Summary of Key Points

1. In ultimate objective terms there is no such thing as 'good' or 'bad'- in practice good is a purely human construct that denotes 'beneficial to some humans'.

2. Action generally involves change - change which is good or beneficial for some things but conversely worse for other things.

3. 'Beauty' is not a universal quality but is just something in the mind of the beholder.

4. Language is the man developed vehicle or road along which human experience and even knowledge is communicated and travels but when examined carefully is flawed and imprecise and is certainly not a source of knowledge in itself.

5. A nexus of causality does exist around our environment and at least to some extent can be decoded to our advantage. Yet that nexus of causality is not necessarily infinite either in time or in space and does certainly break down if you go back far enough along it.

6. A substantial degree of causality or at any rate regularity is essential to enable complex life to survive but that regularity need not be and is not universal and can break down very suddenly.

7. Knowledge can be divided into two parts. One part is 'immediate knowledge' which is derived from

extrapolating regularities within the environment or from decoding a nexus of causality. This immediate knowledge is provisional as all patterns of regularity or systems of causality may end at some stage. The other part is 'ultimate knowledge' which is entirely logically derived and is absolute because it could not logically be otherwise. This ultimate knowledge is absolute and secure but very small in quantity and of generally academic rather than practical use.

8. The problem with 'immediate', provisional knowledge is that it is always subject to sudden, even irrational changes. Therefore it cannot reliably be extrapolated for ever and thus cannot answer ultimate questions. So in reality at its boundaries (before most ultimate answers are reached) a 'philosophical black hole' exists beyond which knowledge cannot progress.

9. The 'philosophical black hole' is also widened by the lack of any absolute existence of 'good' or 'purpose' and may be augmented by the lack of precision of the language or communication we use.

10. Some things can be known to exist because they logically must exist and so are not subject to a philosophical black hole. These include the Universe, ourselves (in some form), Space and Time or at least sequence and even colours (through differentiation from

each other) but the exact details or even nature of such things are ultimately uncertain.

11. The principles of knowledge expounded here apply equally to all 'intelligences' be they alien or artificial intelligences as much as to ourselves. This is because all the uncertainties of 'immediate', provisional knowledge causing universal uncertainty and the certainties of logical knowledge are equally applicable to all 'intelligent' entities. No entity can be certain either of the future or of the extent of Space or of its own possible limitations (even though some intelligences may be more advanced in gaining 'immediate', provisional knowledge than other entities).

12. There are limitations upon all 'intelligences' in relation to their inability to be certain of their true relationship to their environment e.g. uncertainty in relation to the distant future or to the limits of Space or the Universe. This is part of 'Universal Uncertainty'. Therefore no entity can legitimately identify even itself, let alone another entity, as God. At its most basic no entity can know for certain that it is not somehow limited in its scope and one of its limitations is that it is unable to see its own limitations. So no monotheistic God can exist.

13. Though some human afterlife is not absolutely disproved, it seems physically unlikely and could never in any event (because of 'universal uncertainty') be legitimately

known, guaranteed nor even supposed to continue eternally.

14. Intelligent life is likely (though not proven) to have arisen through a sequence of drastic qualitative changes that occurred as a result of sundry critical masses occurring, leading to some replication and development of intelligences at perhaps various times and places within the Universe.

15. There inherently cannot be any overall purpose to the Universe. So no underlying ultimate purpose is possible.

16. Logic is universal and unitary in its truth. Yet even if that improbably and implausibly were not so, 'universal uncertainty' would still apply and would still show God does not exist (as the uncertainty would then be even more comprehensive). The only difference that unreliability in Logic would bring is the destruction of a priori knowledge (such as the ability to know we exist via 'I think, therefore I exist'). So then instead of most things being in the end completely uncertain and unknowable, all things would in the end be for all entities completely unknowable and uncertain.

17. A multiverse is definitionally wrong and in any event it is improbable that any system of multiverses (or different cosmoses) would avoid much seepage between 'various universes/cosmoses'.

18. Human minds frequently distort things, even Science. It has now been shown that humans are capable of creating false memories in their minds. Likewise people have had a tendency to create false concepts such as God, afterlives, goodness and beauty. People tend to distort flimsy or unreliable pieces of evidence to create (and generally stick with) theories that are pleasing to and compatible with the vagaries and illogical tendencies of human minds. People (even scientists) have a tendency to believe what they want to believe or what it suits them to believe in preference to what is factually true.

19. The relation between human minds and human bodies is properly a topic for physiological research, not for philosophical speculation.

20. Human ethics should be centred around establishing a pragmatic 'modus vivendi' (way of living) appropriate to humans and human society, not around any mythical concept of 'good'.

21. Human political philosophy is more complicated than ethics but should be grounded in human experience and take full account of actual human nature.

22. The Universe is most accurately seen as an implacable changing pattern of various material things, a pattern without feelings and without values permeating through it.